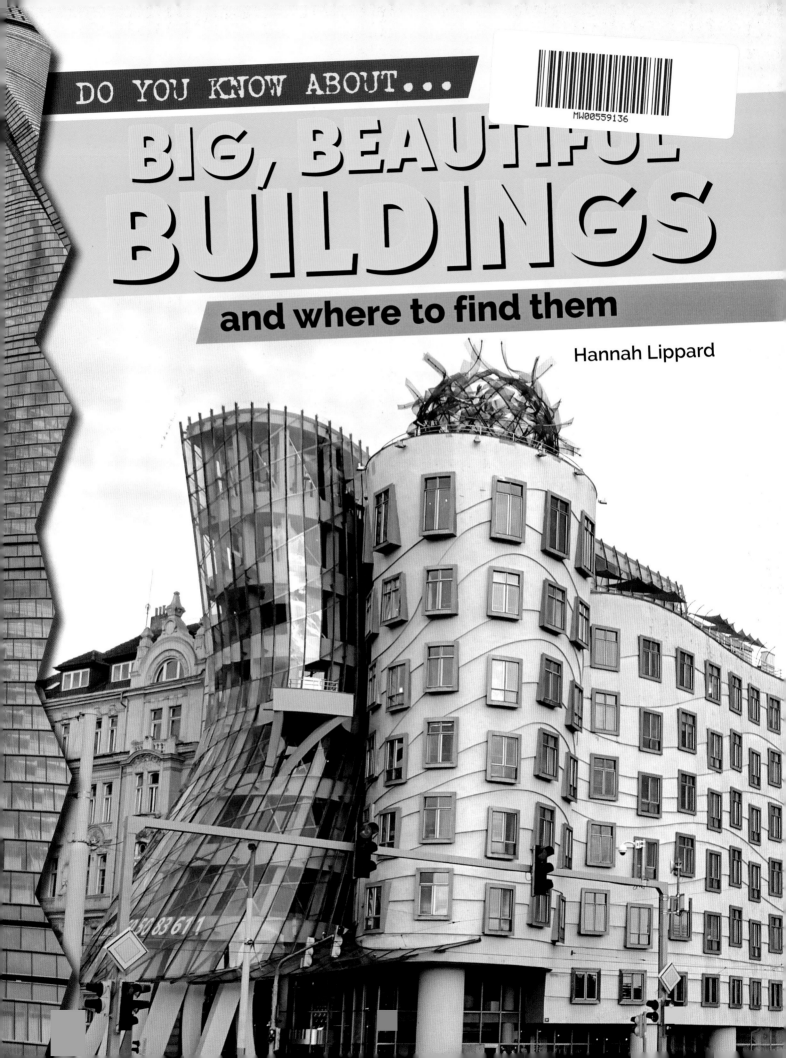

DO YOU KNOW ABOUT...

BIG, BEAUTIFUL BUILDINGS

and where to find them

Hannah Lippard

Photo Credits

Key: (t) top; (tl) top left; (tr) top right; (m) middle; (ml) middle left; (mr) middle right; (b) bottom; (bl) bottom left; (br) bottom right

P6: 30_St_Mary_Axe,_'Gherkin'.jpg (t) Kalabrien_Ricadi_Sandwellen_2129.jpg (ml) Bois_coupe_dans_le_hangar.jpg (mr) 2014_Suchum,_Biuro_Pruratora_Generalnego_Republiki_Abchazji_(03).jpg (b); P7: -2_Femme_Architecte_urbaniste_TOGO.jpg (t) 大工と屋根の垂木構造P8020031.jpg (bl)Workers_on_suspended_scaffold_in_Korolyov.jpg (br); P8: Forbidden_city_-_panoramio.jpg (ml) Reconstructed_Rova_Antananarivo_Madagascar.jpg (mr) Statue_of_Ranavalona_III.jpg (br); P9: Chapel_and_Gabriel_Wing_Palace_of_Versailles.jpg (t) Chateau_de_Versailles_orangerie.jpg (m) Neuschwanstein_throne_room_00180u.jpg (b); P10: Casa_Batllo_Overview_Barcelona_Spain_cut.jpg (m) Fallingwater_-_DSC05598.jpg (bl) Frank_Lloyd_Wright_-_Fallingwater_interior_4.jpg (br); P11: Dancing_House_(7339585566).jpg (t) Ambani_House_July_2010.jpg (b) Praha,_Tancici_dum_v_noci_(1).jpg; P12: Cavalcade_west_frieze_Parthenon_BM.jpg (ml) Luxor-Tempel_09.jpg (mr) Parthenon.jpg (b); P13: Chichen_Itza_3.jpg (t) 2016_Angkor,_Angkor_Wat,_Główna_świątynia_(12).jpg (bl) 2016_Angkor,_Angkor_Wat,_Brama_Angkor_Wat_(05).jpg (br); P14: Kaaba_mirror_edit_jj.jpg (m) Gate_of_Ka-bah.jpg (b); P15: St._Basil_Cathedral.jpg (t) Cupola_del_duomo_di_firenze,_vista,_sinagoga_01.jpg (m) Lotus_temple_in_Delhi,_India.jpg (b); P16: Qin_Shu_Huangdis_grav.jpg (ml) The_Great_Pyramid_of_Giza_(Pyramid_of_Cheops_or_Khufu)_(14823042753).jpg (mr) 1_terracotta_army_2011.jpg (b); P17: Grave_of_Emperor_Jahangir_II.jpg (tl) Facade_and_Entrance_of_Jahangir's_Tomb.jpg (tr) Taj_Mahal,_Agra,_India.jpg (b); P18: Colosseum_in_Rome,_Italy_-_April_2007.jpg (ml) COLLOSSEUM_ROME_Frank_Meier_1.jpg (mr); P19: Moscow-Bolshoi-Theare-1.jpg (t) Teatro_Amazonas_Atualmente_03.jpg (m) London_March_2018._See_profile_for_image_use.IMG_0599.jpg (b); P20: IcelandSymphonyOrchestra_OnStage.jpg (t) 20160527_ViS_8143.jpg (m) 1_The_Opera_House_in_Sydney.jpg (b); P21: Disney_Concert_Hall_by_Carol_Highsmith.jpg (t) The_Mystery_Begins_(5898257465).jpg (m) Harpa_(21460143573).jpg (b); P22: Лувр_-_panoramio_(1).jpg; P23: NationalMuseumofChinapic1.jpg (t) Museo_Soumaya_Plaza.jpg (b); P24: Ottawa_-_ON_-_Library_of_Parliament.jpg (ml) Library_of_Congress_from_North.jpg (mr) James_Madison_Memorial_Building-1.jpg (br) John_Adams_Building_(32084434725).jpg (bl); P25: Biblioteca_nacional_rio_janeiro.jpg (tl) Biblioteca_Nacional_do_Brasil,_hall,_01.jpg (tr) Raza_Library.jpg (b); P26: 20130808_Kings_College_Chapel_01.jpg (ml) Cambridge_-_King's_Chapel_-_stalles.jpg (mr); P27: МГУ,_вид_с_воздуха.jpg (tl) Moscow_05-2012_Mhovaya_05.jpg (tr) NTU_Administration_Building.jpg (ml) NTU_former_administrative_building_front.jpg (mr) Ørestad_Gymnasium_-_inside_(2016).jpg (b); P28: Mauna_Kea_Eastern_Telescopes.jpg (ml) Keck_and_NASA_Telescopes._Mauna_Kea_Summit_(503912)_(21882785511).jpg (ml) NASA's_BARREL_Mission_Halley_Station.jpg (b); P29: Hemispheric_Twilight_-_Valencia,_Spain_-_Jan_2007.jpg (tr) L'Umbracle,_Valencia,_Spain_-_Jan_2007.jpg (tl) NASA's_BARREL_Mission_Launches_20_Balloons.jpg (m) Florida_Polytechnic_University_-_Wide_pano.jpg (bl) Florida_Polytechnic_University_-_Inside.jpg (br); P30: Defense.gov_photo_essay_080723-A-0193C-029.jpg (t) United_States_Capitol_west_front_edit2.jpg (m) London_November_2013-25.jpg (bl) House_of_Lords_2011.jpg (br); P31: Parliament_Building,_Budapest,_outside.jpg (t) Hungarian_Chamber_(6002651590).jpg (m) Romania-1170_-_Palace_of_the_Parliament_(7557749966).jpg (bl) Romania-1361_-_Hallway_(7589089402).jpg (br); P32: Paris_gare_nord_face_3.jpg (ml) Gare_Du_Nord_Interior,_Paris,_France_-_Diliff.jpg (mr) Les_phares_de_lile_Vierge_-_Plouguerneau_-_Finistere_(9596781190).jpg (b); P33: MumbaiAirportT2.jpg (tr) Mumbai_03-2016_114_Airport_international_terminal_interior.jpg (tl) Jeppesen_Terminal_at_DEN_Airport,_north_view,_Aug_2014.jpg (br) Denver_international_airport.jpg (bl); P34: Icehotel_entre_ms.jpg (ml) Icehotel-se-25.jpg (mr) Burj_Al_Arab,_Dubai,_by_Joi_Ito_Dec2007.jpg (br) Burj_al_Arab_lobby_March_2008panod.jpg (bl); P35: FirstWorldHotel_Towers.jpg (tl) Night_View_2.jpg (tr) Marina_Bay_Sands_in_the_evening_-_20101120.jpg (b); P36: French_Laundry_01.jpg (ml) Inside_The_French_Laundry_(19138302550).jpg (mr) Xihulou_02.jpg (bl) Xihulou_47.jpg (br); P37: Ithaa_inside.jpg (t) Inside_El_Celler_de_Can_Roca_(15686799819).jpg (bl) Inside_the_El_Celler_de_Can_Roca_kitchen_(15253163293).jpg (br); P38: 中國昆明521.jpg (m) Torre_di_pisa,_scala_interna_01.jpg (bl) The_Leaning_Tower_of_Pisa_SB.jpg (br); P39: Jam_afghan_architecture_inside_structure.jpg (tl) Minaret_of_jam_2009_ghor.jpg (tr) Eiffel_Tower_2,_15_September_2012.jpg (bl) The_Seine_as_seen_from_the_Eiffel_Tower,_Paris_14_June_2014.jpg (br); P40: Carlton_Centre_2.jpg (tl) New_York_City_Empire_State_Building_entrance_hall_02.jpg (ml) NYC_Empire_State_Building.jpg (mr) 台北101大樓Lo_around_-_panoramio_-_Tianmu_peter_(29).jpg (b); P41: Skypoint_Observation_Deck_4.jpg (t) Gran_Torre_Santiago,_Costanera_Center_(24847266437).jpg (b) NYC_Empire_State_Building.jpg; P42: Emirates_-_panoramio_(82).jpg (m) Final_circulation_of_the_Kaaba.jpg (tl) Ajyad,_Mecca_24231,_Saudi_Arabia_-_panoramio.jpg (tr) Shanghai,_China,_December_2015_-_044.jpg (bl) Shanghai_Shanghai_Tower_5166304.jpg (br) Dubai_-_United_Arab_Emirates_-_panoramio_(42).jpg

www.FlowerpotPress.com
CHC-0912-0479
ISBN: 978-1-4867-1883-2
Made in China/Fabriqué en Chine

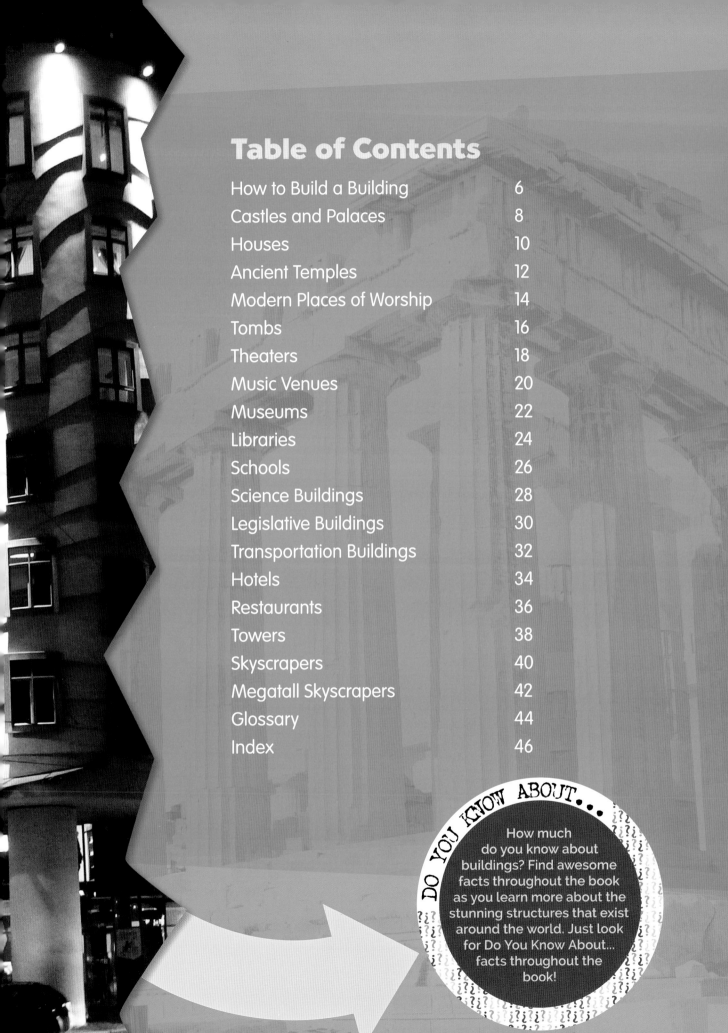

Table of Contents

DO YOU KNOW ABOUT...

How much do you know about buildings? Find awesome facts throughout the book as you learn more about the stunning structures that exist around the world. Just look for Do You Know About... facts throughout the book!

How to Build a Building

A building is a structure created by humans. It usually has walls and a roof and stays permanently in one place. People live, work, and gather in buildings every day. Building a building requires two main steps: design and construction. The art and science of the design and construction of a building is called architecture.

Building Materials

Different buildings are made of different materials. Some materials can be found in nature. These include mud, snow, sand, stone, wood, and grass. Other materials are human-made. These include bricks, concrete, fabric, glass, metal, plastic, and ceramics. Often, different materials are combined to construct a stronger building.

Wood

Sand

DO YOU KNOW ABOUT...

Material Superpowers

Different building materials have special properties that make them useful for different jobs. For example, mud and clay provide natural temperature control. Mud and clay buildings are cool in the summer and warm in the winter. Rock and stone are very heavy and strong, so they typically last longer than any other building material. Glass is transparent, so it keeps the people in a building safe from bad weather while still letting light inside.

Architects

Before a building can be built, it has to be designed. A person who designs buildings is called an architect. An architect has to think about many things at once: how to make the building look nice, how to make it safe and accessible for different kinds of people, how to make it environmentally friendly, and how to make it serve a specific purpose. Most buildings begin as an architect's sketch! Architects also often oversee the construction of buildings they design.

Construction Workers

A construction worker is a person who physically builds a building. There are many different types of construction workers. Carpenters work with building materials like wood using tools like hammers, drills, and saws. Electricians install electrical equipment like wires and switches. Masons lay materials like bricks and concrete on top of each other and then glue them together. Plumbers install plumbing equipment like pipes and fixtures. Welders use powerful tools to heat materials like metal or plastic so they connect to each other.

Castles and Palaces

A castle is a building that is fortified to protect itself from attacks, and a palace is a building where the leader of a country lives. Sometimes people use the words interchangeably and some buildings meet both definitions. Castles and palaces are often extravagantly decorated and extremely large. They may contain multiple buildings that form a complex.

Forbidden City

Location: Beijing, China
Years built: 1406-1420 CE
The Forbidden City is a palace complex that was used by twenty-four different Chinese emperors from 1420 to 1911. It was named the Forbidden City because only the emperor and the emperor's family, servants, and officials were allowed inside. The complex is surrounded by a tall wall and a wide moat to keep intruders out. There are almost 1,000 buildings inside! The largest building, located in the southern part of the complex, is called the Hall of Supreme Harmony. To build the Forbidden City, enormous stones had to be moved to its location. One of these stones weighed over 330 tons (299,371 kilograms).

Rova of Antananarivo

Location: Antananarivo, Madagascar
Years built: 1610-1625 CE
A rova is a Malagasy fortified palace complex. The Rova of Antananarivo was the palace of the rulers of Madagascar from the 1600s to the 1800s. It was built on a hill high above the city. The largest building in the complex is the Queen's Palace, or Manjakamiadana. It was built out of wood for Queen Ranavalona I. Later it was encased in stone for Queen Ranavalona II. The palace was destroyed by a fire in 1995 and then rebuilt. Some buildings in the complex survived the fire, including parts of the Royal Chapel.

Queen Ranavalona III Statue

8

Palace of Versailles

Location: Versailles, France
Years built: 1623-1710 CE

The Palace of Versailles began as a small retreat for the French king Louis XIII. The next king, Louis XIV, had it expanded into a huge palace complex. The royal family lived in apartments on the first floor of the U-shaped main building. The palace also contains a room called the Hall of Mirrors. It is over 230 feet (70.1 meters) long and it has seventeen huge decorated mirrors facing seventeen windows. The ceiling is painted with images from Louis XIV's reign, and the walls are decorated with statues and reliefs. Other buildings in the palace complex include the Royal Chapel and the Royal Opera.

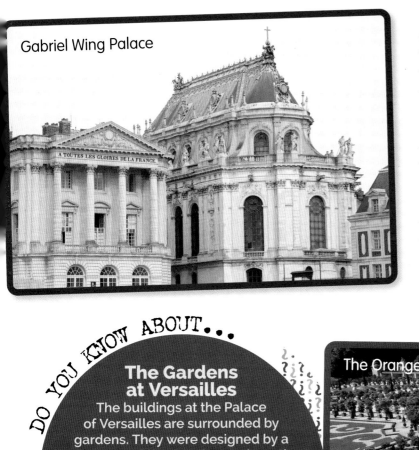

Gabriel Wing Palace

DO YOU KNOW ABOUT...

The Gardens at Versailles

The buildings at the Palace of Versailles are surrounded by gardens. They were designed by a landscape architect. In the gardens, there is a waterway called the Grand Canal that visitors can travel down in little boats. There are also fountains that depict Greek gods and mythical creatures. There is a grove of tropical trees including palm trees, lemon trees, and orange trees. There are paths lined with shrubs and decorated with statues.

The Orangery

Neuschwanstein Castle

Location: Hohenschwangau, Germany
Years built: 1869-1892 CE

Neuschwanstein Castle was commissioned by Ludwig II. Ludwig was the king of Bavaria, a state in Germany. Neuschwanstein Castle was designed like a medieval castle, but it was not built for defense. It was built in honor of the German composer Richard Wagner, and the fourth floor is decorated with paintings of characters from Wagner's operas. The castle has a two-story throne room and an artificial cave. It was the inspiration for the Disney Sleeping Beauty Castle!

Throne Room

Houses

A house is a building where people live, like a castle or palace. Houses are usually smaller than castles and built for just one or two families. But some houses are so large that today they can be used as museums or hotels instead of dwelling places.

Casa Batlló

Location: Barcelona, Spain
Years built: 1877, 1904-1906 CE
When Casa Batlló was first built, it looked completely different. The Spanish architect Antoni Gaudí redesigned the facade and made many changes to the interior. The facade is multicolored and decorated with ceramic and glass. This design creates a wavelike effect in the sunlight. The curved roof has tiles that look like the scales of a dragon. Inside the building are features like stained glass windows, wavy ceilings, dramatic arches, and a brightly lit atrium. The owners of Casa Batlló use the house for events and for tourist visits.

Fallingwater

Location: Pennsylvania, United States
Years built: 1936-1939 CE
Fallingwater was designed by the American architect Frank Lloyd Wright. It was originally built for a family to live in during the summer, but today it is a popular museum. Fallingwater is famous for the way the architecture is integrated with nature. The house is built over a small waterfall in a stream, and it incorporates naturally existing rock into its structure. There are glass walls so that the outside environment is visible.

Dancing House

Location: Prague, Czech Republic
Years built: 1992-1996 CE
The design of the Dancing House was a collaboration between two architects: Vlado Milunic', who is Croatian-Czech, and Frank Gehry, who is Canadian-American. The building was built in the same place where an earlier house was destroyed by bombs during World War II. The Dancing House got its nickname because it has two main parts that look like a dancing couple, specifically Ginger Rogers and Fred Astaire. It is made of concrete and glass. Today, the building contains a hotel.

DO YOU KNOW ABOUT...

Frank Lloyd Wright

Frank Lloyd Wright created 1,114 designs during his career. He was known for two architectural styles. The first was called Prairie style. These buildings were long and low to fit in with a prairie environment. There were not many walls on the inside, to encourage people to spend time together. The second style was called Usonian. These houses were smaller and simpler. Wright designed them in different ways for clients with different needs.

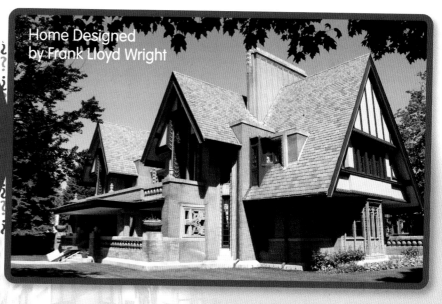

Home Designed by Frank Lloyd Wright

Antilia

Location: Mumbai, India
Years built: 2006-2010 CE
Antilia is a huge house belonging to the richest person in India and his family. It has twenty-seven stories and is 550 feet (167.6 meters) tall. The building is made mostly out of steel and concrete. In addition to rooms most houses have like bedrooms and bathrooms, Antilia has lounges, a ballroom with crystal chandeliers, parking lots, nine elevators, and three helipads. Antilia is not a popular building in India. Many people feel it is insensitive and unfair. The house is worth approximately two billion dollars.

Ancient Temples

A temple is a building where people practice their religion or worship their god or gods. The temples in this section are very old buildings that are no longer used for their original purposes. Today they are mostly sites for scientific study and tourism.

Luxor Temple

Location: Luxor, Egypt
Years built: approximately 1400 BCE
Luxor Temple is a large temple complex near the Nile River. It was built to the ancient Egyptian gods Amual, Mut, and Khonsu. Luxor Temple was begun by Amenhotep III, an Egyptian pharaoh. The construction of the complex continued under later pharaohs, including Ramses II. Luxor Temple is made of sandstone. It consists of halls, chambers, and courtyards surrounded by columns. In front of the large entrance, obelisks and statues of the pharaoh were built. Some of the statues and one of the obelisks can still be seen today.

Marble Frieze

Parthenon

Location: Athens, Greece
Years built: 447-432 BCE
The Parthenon is a temple dedicated to Athena. Athena is the ancient Greek goddess of wisdom, war, and handicraft. The Parthenon is made from white marble and consists of a base, a roof, and sixty-nine (total) columns (though not all the columns are still standing). The temple was decorated with sculptures and carvings of battles and gods. Over the years, some of the sculptures have been relocated to museums. Inside the Parthenon, there used to be a gold and ivory statue of Athena. It has since been lost. There is a modern replica of the Parthenon and its statue in Nashville, Tennessee.

El Castillo, Chichen Itza

Location: Tinum Municipality, Mexico

Years built: approximately 800s-1100s CE

El Castillo is a temple dedicated to Kukulkan, a Maya feathered serpent deity. It is located in the ancient Maya city of Chichen Itza. The building is a limestone pyramid with nine stacked layers and a throne room on the top. Inside the throne room is a red throne shaped like a jaguar. El Castillo is almost one hundred feet (30.48 meters) high. Each side of the pyramid has a staircase. The total number of steps is 365, the same as the number of days in one year. Today, Chichen Itza is an archaeological site. Researchers study the construction of El Castillo and visitors can walk around the building.

DO YOU KNOW ABOUT...

Types of Stone

Each of these four temples is made of stone. Luxor Temple and Angkor Wat were built from sandstone. Sandstone is a sedimentary rock, meaning it is made up of sediment. The sediment in sandstone is sand. El Castillo was built from limestone. Limestone is white and made up of the remains of animals, like shells. The Parthenon is actually also made of limestone—marble is a type of limestone that is crystallized and can be polished.

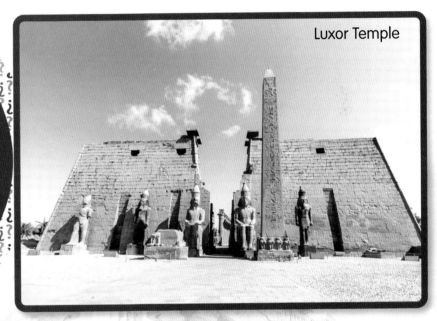

Luxor Temple

Vishnu Statue

Angkor Wat

Location: Angkor, Cambodia

Years built: approximately 1100s CE

Angkor Wat is a huge temple complex that covers about 500 acres (2 square kilometers) of land. It was originally a Hindu temple and later became a Buddhist temple. Angkor Wat is bordered by a wide, deep moat. The buildings in the complex are made of sandstone. At the center, there is a 213-foot-tall (64.9 meters) tower surrounded by four shorter towers. The tall right side tower contains a statue of the Hindu god Vishnu at the top. Archaeologists continue to make discoveries on the site. Some recent finds include hidden paintings, a sand structure, houses where temple workers lived, and a chamber underneath the main tower.

Modern Places of Worship

The places of worship in this section were all constructed or expanded during the past 500 years. To some extent, they are all still used for religious purposes today. Some of them are also museums.

Great Mosque of Mecca

Location: Mecca, Saudi Arabia
Years built: approximately 2130 BCE-Present
The Great Mosque of Mecca is a Muslim place of worship. It consists of a large courtyard surrounded by covered areas for prayer. In the courtyard is a building called the Kaaba. The Kaaba is a shrine made out of stone and usually covered with a huge piece of fabric. On the corner of the Kaaba is a black stone. Muslims believe this stone was given to Adam and Eve, the first humans. The Great Mosque is so large that it can hold up to over one million people at a time! Millions of people travel to the mosque every year in a journey called a pilgrimage.

DO YOU KNOW ABOUT...

When Was the Mosque Built?
According to the Quran, the holy book of Islam, the construction of the Great Mosque of Mecca began with Abraham, an important figure in Islam as well as Judaism and Christianity. This would have taken place around 2130 BCE. In the 600s and 700s CE, the mosque was expanded. Taller walls, ceilings, columns, and a minaret were built. In the 1620s, the mosque was damaged by rain and flooding. It had to be rebuilt, and it is still being renovated and expanded today.

Kaaba

Saint Basil's Cathedral

Location: Moscow, Russia
Years built: 1555-1561 CE
Saint Basil's Cathedral is a Russian Orthodox church, a denomination of Christianity. It consists of a tall nave in the center surrounded by nine smaller chapels, which correspond to points on a compass. Originally, Saint Basil's Cathedral was probably white with gold domes. The colorful paint was not added until the 1600s. There are still church services in the cathedral sometimes, but now it mainly functions as a museum.

Great Synagogue of Florence

Location: Florence, Italy
Years built: 1874-1882 CE
The Great Synagogue of Florence is a Jewish house of worship. The facade is pink and white stone. The domes are covered in copper, and the doors are made of walnut wood. Inside, there are walls decorated in geometric patterns and gold. The synagogue also has stained glass windows and marble floors. In addition to being a place of worship, the Great Synagogue of Florence includes a museum and cultural center.

Lotus Temple

Location: Delhi, India
Years built: 1978-1986 CE
The Lotus Temple is a house of worship of the Bahá'í Faith. It is open to people of all religions. The temple is made of white marble. It was designed in the shape of a lotus flower with twenty-seven petals. The architect Fariborz Sahba chose the lotus because it is a symbol shared by different religions in India, such as Hinduism and Buddhism. The design and construction of the building involved about 800 people. The Lotus Temple has nine sides, each with its own entrance. Surrounding the building are nine pools of water that represent the flower's leaves.

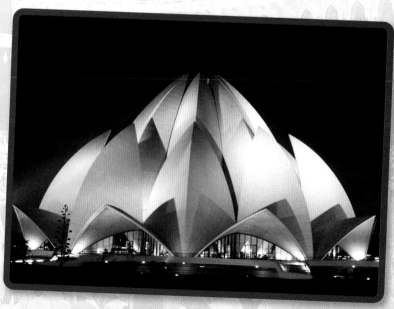

Tombs

A tomb is a place where people are buried after they have died. Some tombs are built above ground, and some tombs are built underground. Large tombs are sometimes called mausoleums. The tombs in this section were built for royalty.

Great Pyramid of Giza

Location: Giza, Egypt
Years built: approximately 2580-2560 BCE
The Great Pyramid of Giza is one of three pyramids in Giza. It is the largest and oldest of the three. It was probably built as a tomb for the pharaoh Khufu. The Great Pyramid is 481 feet (146.6 meters) tall. It is made of about 2.3 million extremely heavy blocks of stone. The walls inside are covered in art and inscriptions. Archaeologists are still not sure exactly how the pyramid was built. The construction would have required a lot of strength and precision.

Terra-cotta Soldiers

Mausoleum of the First Qin Emperor

Location: Xi'an, China
Years built: approximately 246-208 BCE
The Mausoleum of the First Qin Emperor is the underground tomb of Qin Shi Huang. Qin Shi Huang was the first emperor of China. The mausoleum is a necropolis, a large, ancient cemetery with many structures. Archaeologists have excavated part of the necropolis. But they have not yet excavated the tomb itself, which is buried under a hill. The emperor's tomb is surrounded by an army of thousands of life-size soldiers made from a type of clay called terra-cotta. So far, archaeologists have found 2,000 terra-cotta warriors. There may be more than 6,000 left. Each soldier has unique facial features and clothing.

Tomb of Jahangir

Location: Lahore, Pakistan
Years built: 1627-1637 CE

The Tomb of Jahangir is a mausoleum built for Emperor Jahangir, the fourth Mughal emperor. The Mughal Empire included India, Pakistan, Afghanistan, and Bangladesh. The tomb is surrounded by four gardens and many fountains. The roof of the tomb is flat, but there are four minarets at the corners.
The tomb chamber itself is shaped like an octagon. Inside is a cenotaph, an empty monument that is shaped like a coffin but does not contain the emperor's remains. Jahangir is actually buried in a crypt beneath the cenotaph.

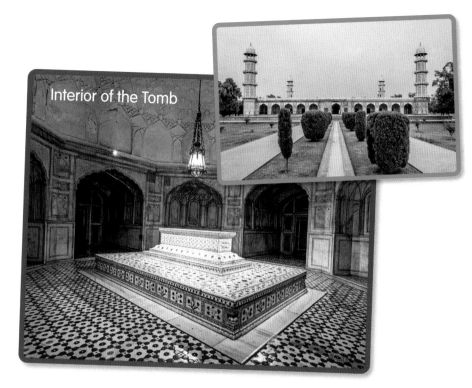

Interior of the Tomb

DO YOU KNOW ABOUT...

Will the Tomb Ever Be Opened?

Archaeologists have not accessed the place where Qin Shi Huang is buried because they could damage the tomb. Another challenge is that the tomb may be surrounded by liquid mercury. Mercury can be poisonous to humans, so this would be very dangerous for the explorers. But technology is constantly improving. One day people may be able to see inside the tomb using robots instead of humans.

Mercury

Taj Mahal

Location: Agra, India
Years built: approximately 1632-1653 CE

The Taj Mahal is a mausoleum complex. It was commissioned by the fifth Mughal emperor for his wife Mumtaz Mahal. The Taj Mahal is made of white marble, as well as stones like jade, crystal, and turquoise for decoration. Over 20,000 construction workers built the mausoleum. In addition to the tomb building, the Taj Mahal complex includes a garden and several structures made of red sandstone: a gateway, a mosque, and a jawab (a building that is like a copy of the mosque). The Taj Mahal is a very popular tourist destination. Tens of thousands of people visit the Taj Mahal most days.

Theaters

A theater is a building where dramatic performances or spectacles are shown, such as plays, operas, and ballets. The word "theater" can also refer to a building where movies are shown.

Colosseum

Location: Rome, Italy
Years built: approximately 72-80 CE
The Colosseum is an amphitheater made out of stone. It was the largest amphitheater of its time. The Colosseum has three stories with many entrances formed by arched columns. More than 50,000 people could have sat inside. Plays were not the form of entertainment enjoyed at the Colosseum. The Romans watched fights with gladiators, wild animals, and ships. Gladiators even participated in mock naval battles.

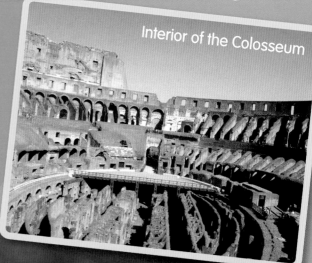

Interior of the Colosseum

DO YOU KNOW ABOUT...
Types of Classical Columns

The type of column was different on each level of the Colosseum: Doric on the bottom, Ionic in the middle, and Corinthian on the top. Doric columns are the most simple. Ionic columns are narrower than Doric columns. The top of an Ionic column, called the capital, is shaped like a scroll. Corinthian columns are the most complicated. The capital is carved to look like leaves or flowers.

DORIC   IONIC   CORINTHIAN

Bolshoi Theatre

Location: Moscow, Russia
Years built: 1821-1825 CE
The Bolshoi Theatre hosts opera and ballet performances. The exterior of the building has a portico with eight columns and a sculpture of the Greek god Apollo riding in a chariot on the top. The auditorium of the theater holds nearly 2,300 people. In 1853, a fire almost completely burned down the Bolshoi Theatre. After its reconstruction, it was bigger, and the acoustics of the auditorium were improved.

Amazon Theatre

Location: Manaus, Brazil
Years built: 1884-1896 CE
The Amazon Theatre is an opera house. It is a Renaissance-style building. Many of the materials to build the theater came from Europe: ceramic tiles from France, marble from Italy, and steel from Scotland. The colorful tiles on the dome on the roof form the Brazilian flag. There are 36,000 tiles in all. Inside the theater are 198 chandeliers! The curtain on the stage is painted to depict two rivers meeting to form the Amazon River. In addition to opera, the Amazon Theatre has orchestral performances and shows films every year during the Amazonas Film Festival.

Shakespeare's Globe

Location: England, United Kingdom
Years built: 1991-1997 CE
Shakespeare's Globe is a replica of the Globe Theatre. The Globe Theatre was built in 1599 by the playwright William Shakespeare's acting company. Shakespeare's plays were performed there. The original Globe Theatre was destroyed in 1644. Archaeologists helped design the replica by studying the foundations of the original building. The construction workers mostly used building materials and methods from Shakespeare's time. Shakespeare's Globe helps performers and researchers learn about how Shakespeare's plays were performed.

Music Venues

A venue is a place where a specific kind of event occurs. Music venues are buildings where music is performed. Some music venues are used for specific types of music, and others are more general.

Musikverein

Location: Vienna, Austria
Years built: 1867-1870 CE

The Musikverein is a large concert hall where classical music is performed. The building has multiple halls, some for performance and some for rehearsal.
The largest room is the Golden Hall, also called the Great Hall. It has 1,744 seats for the audience. It is called a shoebox hall because it is shaped like a rectangle. The Golden Hall has excellent acoustics because of its shape and high ceiling.
The Musikverein was designed in a Greek style. It has Ionic columns, statues on its facade, and Greek mythical figures painted on the ceiling of the Golden Hall.

DO YOU KNOW ABOUT...

Opera House Financing

The Sydney Opera House was originally estimated to cost $7 million AUD. By the time it was completed, the project ended up costing about $102 million AUD and was ultimately funded by the state lottery. Not only was the cost of the project underestimated, so was the time it would take to be completed. The original estimate was four years, but it ultimately took fourteen years.

Sydney Opera House

Location: Sydney, Australia
Years built: 1959-1973 CE

The Sydney Opera House is a performing arts center that includes multiple venues. There is a concert hall and a recording studio as well as multiple theaters and an area for outdoor performances. The roof of the Sydney Opera House is made up of concrete shells. Each shell comes from one imaginary sphere. The building was designed by the Danish architect Jørn Utzon. He won an international contest to design an opera house for Australia.

Walt Disney Concert Hall

Location: California, United States
Years built: 1999-2003 CE

Walt Disney Concert Hall was designed by Frank Gehry, one of the architects who designed Dancing House. The outside of the building is made of steel and looks like curved sails. Inside, the walls, seats, and stage are made from wood. There are 2,265 seats. There are no balconies or prosceniums. This is so the orchestra and the audience are not as separated from each other. Walt Disney Concert Hall has two resident companies: the Los Angeles Philharmonic (an orchestra) and the Los Angeles Master Chorale (a chorus).

DO YOU KNOW ABOUT...

Harpa's Facade

Harpa's facade is made up of 9,211 windows. On one side of the building the windows are not flat. They are glass tubes shaped like hexagons. Most of the panels are translucent, but some are colorful or reflective. The facade interacts with light to make patterns inside the building and reflect visitors.

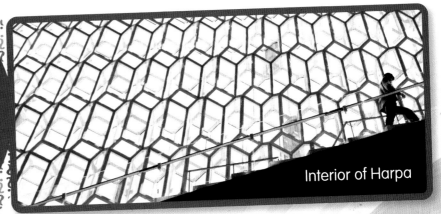

Interior of Harpa

Harpa

Location: Reykjavik, Iceland
Years built: 2007-2011 CE

Harpa is a concert hall where a variety of music is performed. There are three resident companies: an orchestra, an opera, and a band. The building also hosts music festivals and visiting companies from other countries. Harpa's many windows offer a view of the ocean and mountains. The inside walls are made of dark red concrete. Both the concrete and the glass are meant to symbolize lava.

Museums

A museum is a place where objects are stored so they can be viewed and studied. Objects on display in museums are called exhibits.

Louvre Museum

Location: Paris, France
Years built: approximately 1100s-1200s CE

The Louvre is the largest art museum in the world. It was originally built as a castle to protect Paris. It became a museum in 1793. At first, the Louvre had less than 600 paintings. Today, the museum displays over 35,000 works of art at a time. It is too large to see all the art in one visit. The Louvre has an underground lobby with a glass pyramid above the ground and an upside-down glass pyramid on the ceiling. Over eight million people visit the museum each year. One of the most famous works of art in the museum is the painting *Mona Lisa* by Leonardo da Vinci.

Smithsonian Institution

Location: Washington, DC, United States
Years built: 1846-1855 CE

The Smithsonian Institution is a complex of nineteen museums. It is the largest museum complex in the world. Eleven of the Smithsonian's museums are located on the National Mall, a park in Washington, DC, with many monuments, memorials, and museums. Some of the Smithsonian's museums are the African American Museum, the Air and Space Museum, the American Indian Museum, and the Natural History Museum.

National Museum of China

Location: Beijing, China
Years built: 1912-1959 CE

The National Museum of China is the largest museum in China and one of the largest in the world. It has over one million objects, including bone replicas, tools, art, and pottery. It is a merger of two smaller museums: the National Museum of Chinese History and the National Museum of Chinese Revolution. From 2007 to 2010, the museum building was expanded and renovated. It is now almost three times as big and covers more than two million square feet (185,806.1 square meters).

DO YOU KNOW ABOUT...

National Air and Space Museum

The main building of the Air and Space Museum has twenty-one different galleries with hundreds of objects on display, including real aircraft and spacecraft. The museum also has its own planetarium and IMAX theater with a movie screen five stories high.

National Air and Space Museum

Museo Soumaya

Location: Mexico City, Mexico
Years built: 1994-2011 CE

The Museo Soumaya is an art museum with two buildings and 66,000 pieces of art. Most of the art is Central American or European. Carlos Slim, the wealthiest person in Mexico, donated the art and paid for the buildings. The older building is in an area of Mexico City called Plaza Loreto, and the newer building is in an area called Plaza Carso. The Plaza Carso building is six stories tall and it has a complicated exterior made out of 16,000 hexagons of aluminum.

Libraries

A library is a place that keeps collections of items, especially reference materials like books. People can use the items in libraries for research or entertainment, but they cannot buy them or keep them forever. Many libraries allow people to borrow books, but sometimes books can only be consulted at the library.

Library of Parliament

Location: Ottawa, Canada
Years built: 1859-1876 CE
The Library of Parliament is a research library for the Parliament of Canada. It contains about 650,000 items. The building is shaped like a circle and has flying buttresses on the outside. The roofing is made of copper. The inside is paneled with white pinewood and decorated with carvings. The library uses a system of temperature and humidity control to preserve the books.

Library of Congress

Location: Washington, DC, United States
Years built: 1897-1938 CE
The Library of Congress is the biggest library in the world. It is a research library for the US Congress. It contains more than 164 million items in about 838 miles (1348.6 kilometers) of bookshelves. Over half of the books in the Library of Congress are in languages other than English. The library has three buildings and twenty-two reading rooms. It was founded in 1800 but the first building was built in 1897. The later buildings were built in 1939, 1976, and 2007.

John Adams Building

James Madison Memorial Building

Biblioteca Nacional

Location: Rio de Janeiro, Brazil
Years built: 1905-1910 CE

Biblioteca Nacional or the National Library of Brazil has a main building that holds about nine million items and five annex buildings holding an additional six million items. Every time something is published in Brazil, one copy has to be sent to the National Library. The library receives hundreds of donations a day. It also has a collection of 21,742 photographs from the 1800s.

DO YOU KNOW ABOUT...

The Oldest Library

The oldest library in the world is possibly the Ebla Library. It was the royal library of the ancient kingdom of Ebla in Syria. It was built between 2500 and 2250 BCE. Today, the library is in ruins. Archaeologists have found thousands of clay tablets with writing on them. They may have been stored on shelves and arranged by subject, like in modern libraries.

Rampur Raza Library

Location: Rampur, India
Years built: late 1700s CE

The Rampur Raza Library was founded in 1774 by the ruler of Rampur. The first items in the library were the royal family's collection of manuscripts, palm leaves, and paintings. The Rampur Raza Library moved to its current building in 1957. This building was originally part of a palace. Today it is managed by the Indian government. The Rampur Raza Library has about 60,000 books and 17,000 manuscripts. The texts are in many different languages spoken in India: Arabic, Urdu, Persian, Turkish, Pashto, Sanskrit, and Hindi.

Schools

Schools are buildings where people go to learn. Some of the people in a school are students, and others are teachers. Different schools are for different levels of education.

University of Cambridge

Location: England, United Kingdom
Years built: 1209 CE

The University of Cambridge contains thirty-one different colleges. Some of the most famous buildings in the university are King's College Chapel and the history faculty building. Construction of King's College Chapel began in 1446 and took more than fifty years to build. It has large stained glass windows and a tall ceiling. The history faculty building was finished much later, in 1968. At the center of the building is a large library surrounded by offices. The building is made of concrete, brick, glass, and steel.

King's Chapel

DO YOU KNOW ABOUT...

Universities

A university is a type of school offering higher education, or the level of education after primary (such as elementary school) and secondary (such as high school) education. People graduate from universities with degrees in specific areas, like art or math.

University of Kansas

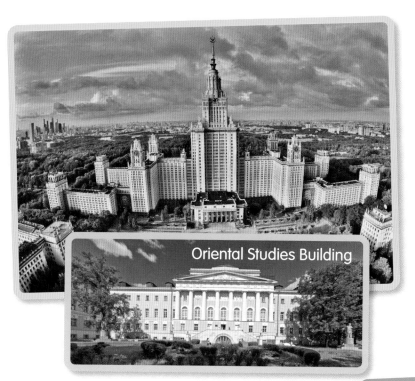

Lomonosov Moscow State University

Location: Moscow, Russia
Years built: 1755 CE-Present

Lomonosov Moscow State University is the largest and oldest university in Russia. It focuses on science and mathematics. It has several observatories and over 350 laboratories. The tower of the main building of the university is nearly 800 feet (243.8 meters) tall. It has thirty-six stories and more than 5,000 rooms. The star on the top of the tower weighs twelve tons (10.9 tonnes). The main building is one of the tallest buildings in Europe.

Oriental Studies Building

Nanyang Technological University

Location: Jurong West, Singapore
Years built: 1981 CE-Present

Nanyang Technological University has eight colleges and schools where students study engineering, science, the humanities, arts and social sciences, business, and medicine. Many of the buildings have an environmentally-friendly design. For example, the building of the School of Art, Design, and Media has reflective glass walls and a grass-covered roof. The Hive, a building with classrooms and community areas, has a special ventilation system that keeps the building cool while saving energy.

Front of Administrative Building

Ørestad Gymnasium

Location: Copenhagen, Denmark
Years built: 2007 CE

Ørestad Gymnasium is a high school designed to encourage collaboration. There are no classrooms, so that students can see what activities other students are doing. The outer walls are made of glass. The teaching materials are entirely digital, including computers and tablets. This allows students to participate in the same class even when in different areas of the school. The architecture is meant to encourage a balance between independent learning and learning led by teachers.

Science Buildings

Some buildings are designed for scientific purposes. People use these buildings for research, entertainment, or education.

Mauna Kea Observatories

Location: Mauna Kea, Hawaii
Years built: 1967-2012 CE

The Mauna Kea Observatories is a place where astronomers study the sky. They use huge telescopes to view objects and events in space. The observatory is located on top of a dormant volcano. Mauna Kea is at such a high elevation that it is above 40 percent of the planet's atmosphere. The top of the volcano is usually higher than clouds. This means that the view from Mauna Kea is clearer than from any other observatory on Earth. Mauna Kea Observatories has two of the largest telescopes in the world, the Keck telescopes, which have thirty-three-foot (10.1 meters) mirrors.

Halley Research Station

Location: Brunt Ice Shelf, Antarctica
Years built: 1956-2013 CE

Halley Research Station is a facility where scientists research topics like climate change, sea level, and weather in space. It is divided into eight separate but connected parts, called modules. The blue modules have places to sleep and work. The red module has places to eat and socialize. Halley Research Station is the first mobile research facility in the world. The modules can be separated and moved to a new location. This is an important ability, because the facility is not located on stable land. The ice of the Brunt Ice Shelf is constantly moving.

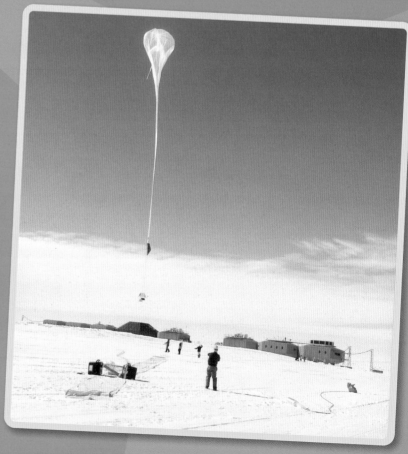

Hemispheric

L'Umbracle

Ciudad de las Artes y las Ciencias

Location: Valencia, Spain
Years built: 1996-2005 CE

Ciudad de las Artes y las Ciencias or the City of Arts and Sciences is a complex of education and entertainment buildings. The first building in the complex was the Hemispheric, which resembles a giant human eye. The sphere inside the Hemispheric is a theater where people can watch astronomical projections and other shows. Another important building is the Science Museum, which resembles the skeleton of a whale. It has interactive exhibits, workshops, and demonstrations. Other buildings combine science and art. For example, the L'Umbracle contains a sculpture gallery and garden.

DO YOU KNOW ABOUT...

Antarctic Climate

Halley Research Station has to withstand extreme cold and darkness. In the winter, temperatures can range from -4 degrees Fahrenheit (-20 C) to -67 (-55 C). For more than one hundred days of the year, it is constantly dark. To deal with the weather, each module of the research station has special legs that can raise it above the snow.

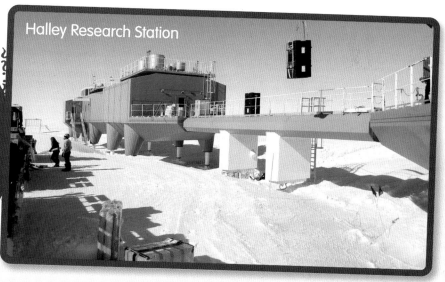
Halley Research Station

Florida Polytechnic IST Building

Location: Florida, United States
Years built: 2011-2014 CE

The Innovation, Science, and Technology (or IST) Building is the main building of Florida Polytechnic University. It contains twenty-six classrooms, eleven laboratories, an auditorium, a cafe, a huge common room, and offices. The IST Building is shaped like an oval. Its roof is a white dome that can change position so the second floor receives light as the sun moves throughout the day. The IST Building was designed by the Spanish architect Santiago Calatrava, who also designed the City of Arts and Sciences

Interior of IST Building

Legislative Buildings

A legislature is a branch of a country's government. It is a group of people who make and change the laws for the country. Legislative buildings are places where the legislature meets to discuss and vote on laws. Some legislatures are bicameral, which means they have two parts, often called houses or chambers. Others are unicameral, which means they have only one house.

United States Capitol

Location: Washington, DC, United States
Years built: 1793-1800 CE

The United States Capitol is the place where the United States Congress meets. There are two houses of Congress: the House of Representatives and the Senate. The Capitol is located on the National Mall, like many of the Smithsonian museums. The top of the building has a white dome. The Capitol has five floors, miles of hallways, and more than 600 rooms. The House of Representatives and the Senate meet in chambers on the second floor. This floor also has a circular public area with art on display called the Rotunda.

Palace of Westminster

Location: England, United Kingdom
Years built: 1840-1876 CE

The Palace of Westminster is the place where the Parliament of the United Kingdom meets. Like Congress, Parliament has two houses: the House of Commons and the House of Lords. The original Palace of Westminster was built in the early 11th century but was destroyed by a fire in 1834. The current building was built from limestone with steep iron roofs. The building has three towers. The tallest is called the Victoria Tower, and it is 325 feet (98.5 meters) tall. The most famous is the Elizabeth Tower, which is more often called Big Ben. It has a large clock and a bell.

House of Lords

Hungarian Parliament Building

Location: Budapest, Hungary
Years built: 1885-1902 CE

The Hungarian Parliament Building is the place where the Hungarian parliament, called the National Assembly of Hungary, meets. The National Assembly is unicameral. The Hungarian Parliament Building is the largest building in Hungary and the third largest legislative building in the entire world. It is 879 feet (268 meters) long and 315 feet (96 meters) tall. It has 12.5 miles (20 kilometers) of stairs, ten courtyards, and 691 rooms. The architect who designed the building was inspired by the Palace of Westminster in London.

DO YOU KNOW ABOUT...

Gothic Revival

The Hungarian Parliament Building was built in an architectural style called Gothic Revival. Gothic Revival was popular in the 1800s. It was inspired by the Gothic style, which was popular during the Middle Ages. Gothic Revival was used by people who wanted to recreate the appearance of Gothic architecture, but not for the reasons it was originally used. It was in competition with another style called neoclassicism. Neoclassicism was also a type of revival. It was a revival of the Classical style of ancient Greece and Rome. Neoclassicism is the style of the US Capitol building.

Hungarian Parliament Building Chamber

Palace of the Parliament

Hallway in the Palace of the Parliament

Location: Bucharest, Romania
Years built: 1984-1997 CE

The Palace of the Parliament is the place where the Parliament of Romania meets. The Parliament of Romania has two chambers: the Chamber of Deputies and the Senate. The Palace of the Parliament is the second-largest administrative building in the world. It is also the heaviest building in the world—it weighs over eight billion pounds (more than four billion kilograms). The Palace of the Parliament was designed by a team of hundreds of architects led by head architect Anca Petrescu. She was only twenty-eight at the time she was appointed head architect. The palace is made of marble, steel, bronze, crystal, cement, and wood.

Transportation Buildings

Transportation is movement from one place to another. Usually when people think about transportation, they think of vehicles, like trains, airplanes, and boats. But each of those vehicles relies on buildings to successfully transport people and cargo.

Interior of Gare du Nord

Gare du Nord

Location: Paris, France
Years built: 1861-1889 CE

The Gare du Nord is the busiest train station in Europe. About 200 million people pass through the Gare du Nord every year. The building is neoclassical. Its facade has twenty-three statues that stand for different cities in Europe. The inside of the Gare du Nord is 600 feet (182.9 meters) long. In addition to regular trains, metro trains and buses have stops at the station. The Gare du Nord has forty-four platforms.

Île Vierge Lighthouse

Location: Finistère, France
Years built: 1896-1902 CE

Lighthouses are tall structures with a light at the top that help guide ships when it is dark or hard to see. The Île Vierge Lighthouse is the tallest traditional lighthouse—a lighthouse built with traditional masonry materials—in the world. It is 271 feet (82.5 meters) tall. Its white light flashes every five seconds and can be seen from thirty-one miles (49.9 kilometers) away. The Île Vierge Lighthouse is made of granite, a type of hard rock. Inside there is a spiral staircase with hundreds of steps to reach the top.

Chhatrapati Shivaji Maharaj International Airport

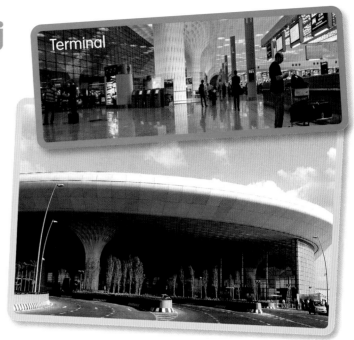

Terminal

Location: Mumbai, India
Years built: 1930-2014 CE
The Chhatrapati Shivaji Maharaj International Airport has three terminals. Terminal 2 covers 4.4 million square feet (408,773.4 square meters). It has four stories, but because of its design, sunlight reaches all the way to the first floor. The facade of the building is a fifty-foot (15.2 meter) glass wall so that people outside the terminal can watch departures. To help passengers move through Terminal 2, there are forty-one moving walkways, forty-seven escalators, and 161 elevators. There is also a hotel and an art museum.

DO YOU KNOW ABOUT...

Airport Terminals
A terminal is an airport building passengers must move through before departure and after arrival. It is an administrative building. Passengers can buy tickets and go through security in a terminal. Terminals also usually have places to shop, eat, and relax. Passengers board a plane through a part of the terminal called the concourse. Other important parts of airports are the runway, where planes land and take off; the control tower, where a controller gives pilots information about weather and traffic; and the hangar, where airplanes are repaired.

Airport Terminal

Denver International Airport

Terminal

Location: Colorado, United States
Years built: 1989 CE-Present
The Denver International Airport is the largest airport in the United States and the second largest in the world. The roof of its terminal is made of white fabric designed to look like snowy mountains. The fabric is translucent, so 10 percent of the sunlight shining on it can pass through the material into the building. The airport also has a solar energy system made up of over 42,614 solar panels.

Hotels

Hotels are buildings where people can sleep and eat. They are often used by travelers. Hotels are like temporary houses where many different people stay at once.

Icehotel

Location: Jukkasjärvi, Sweden
Years built: 1989 CE-Present

The Icehotel is a hotel made out of ice and snow. It is built in the winter and melts in the summer. Therefore, it has to be rebuilt every year. The ice comes from a nearby river, and the water returns to the river when the hotel melts. Artists come to Sweden to create the different rooms of the hotel, so it looks different every year. The temperature in the Icehotel stays below freezing all the time. Guests sleep in special sleeping bags on ice beds. In 2016, a new year-round Icehotel building was built. It uses solar power to keep the ice cold even during the summer.

Interior of the Icehotel

Burj Al Arab Jumeirah

Location: Dubai, United Arab Emirates
Years built: 1994-1999 CE

The Burj Al Arab Jumeirah is one of the tallest hotels in the world. It is more than 1,000 feet (305 meters) tall and it has twenty-eight double stories. It was built on an artificial island and it is shaped like the sail of a ship. The outside of the building is made of concrete and steel. The inside is decorated with gold, carpets, and marble. The atrium of the Burj Al Arab Jumeirah is 600 feet (182.9 meters) high and has a fountain in the center with a waterfall. The hotel is extremely expensive. The largest suite, called the Royal Suite, costs about $24,000 USD (31,748.40 CAD) per night.

First World Hotel and Plaza

Location: Pahang, Malaysia
Years built: 2000 CE-Present

First World Hotel is the largest hotel in the world by number of rooms. It has 7,351 rooms, and more than thirty million guests have stayed there. The rooms are divided between the two towers of the hotel.
First World Hotel was the first hotel in southeast Asia with kiosks allowing guests to check in and out by themselves. In the convention center, there is a ballroom that covers more than 150,000 square feet (13,935.5 square meters). This makes it the largest ballroom in the world without pillars to support it. The plaza includes shopping areas, arcades, restaurants, casinos, and a theme park.

DO YOU KNOW ABOUT...

Land Reclamation

The first few years of construction were not spent building the Burj Al Arab Jumeirah itself. They were spent reclaiming land. Land reclamation is a process where land is created in a body of water. This is usually done by depositing materials like stone and dirt in the area until they rise above the surface of the water.

Marina Bay Sands

Location: Singapore
Years built: 2006-2011 CE

Marina Bay Sands is a resort, a place that offers features like entertainment and shopping as well as lodging and food. In addition to a hotel with thousands of rooms, Marina Bay Sands has a mall, a museum, theaters, restaurants, a casino, and more. The hotel itself has three towers that are each more than fifty stories tall. On top of the towers is a platform called SkyPark. The platform cantilevers on one end, or extends out without a support underneath it. SkyPark is 1,000 feet (305 meters) long and includes a garden and a swimming pool. The museum of Marina Bay Sands is shaped like a lotus flower and has art and science exhibits.

Restaurants

A restaurant is a building where people come to eat. Two important parts of a restaurant are the dining area and the kitchen. The diners sit and eat in the dining area, and the chefs prepare the food in the kitchen.

Dining Room

The French Laundry

Location: California, United States
Years built: approximately 1900s CE
The French Laundry is a French restaurant with American influences. The restaurant was not founded until 1978, but its building was constructed during the 1900s. The building is a cottage with two stories, made from stone and wood. It originally functioned as a saloon, a place like a bar that serves alcohol. Later it was used as a house and a French steam laundry, which is how it got its name. The menu of the restaurant changes every day. Guests are served many small courses, and ingredients are only used once during the entire meal.

West Lake Restaurant

Location: Changsha, China
Years built: 2000-2004 CE
West Lake Restaurant is the biggest Chinese restaurant in the world. It can hold up to 5,000 people. The restaurant has multiple buildings and more than one hundred private dining rooms. Nineteen of the rooms are luxury dining rooms. West Lake Restaurant also has a theater that puts on shows daily and a courtyard with food trucks. There are five kitchens with 300 chefs working in them.

Ithaa

Location: Rangali Island, Maldives
Years built: 2004-2005 CE

Ithaa is a restaurant that is entirely underwater. It is the first undersea restaurant made only of glass. Ithaa is small, and only fourteen people can eat in the building at once; however, the experience feels much larger! The restaurant is surrounded by a coral reef, so animals like fish, turtles, stingrays, and sharks are just outside the glass. Ithaa has been called the most beautiful restaurant in the world.

DO YOU KNOW ABOUT...

Eating Underwater

Ithaa was built above ground in Singapore and then moved to its current location. Ithaa is located sixteen feet (4.9 meters) below sea level. To enter the restaurant, diners walk down a spiral staircase into the glass building. The glass has to be cleaned every day. Because of its location, Ithaa may only last about twenty years.

El Celler de Can Roca

Location: Girona, Spain
Years built: 2007 CE

El Celler de Can Roca has been ranked the best restaurant in the world twice. It originally opened in 1986, but it moved to its current building in 2007. The new building is larger and was built specifically for the restaurant. Forty-five people can eat in El Celler de Can Roca at once. Diners can also take a tour of the kitchen and the wine cellar, which are about the same size. The walls of El Celler de Can Roca are made of glass so people can see the view outside. The restaurant is so popular that people have to make reservations eleven months ahead of time to eat there.

Dining Room

Kitchen

Towers

A tower is a building that is taller than it is wide. It stands out from its surroundings because of its height. You have already read about some towers in this book: a lighthouse is a tower with a light at the top, and some hotels have towers.

Three Pagodas

Location: Dali, China
Years built: approximately 800s-900s CE
A pagoda is a type of East Asian tower. It is tiered, which means it has multiple layers stacked on top of each other. The tiers of a pagoda usually have their own roofs, which curve upward at the ends. The Three Pagodas are part of Chongsheng Temple, a Buddhist temple. The middle pagoda has sixteen tiers and is about 230 feet (70 meters) tall. The other two pagodas have ten tiers and are about 140 feet (42.7 meters) tall. Hundreds of Buddhist artifacts were discovered in the middle pagoda, including statues, documents, coins, and musical instruments. The Three Pagodas are some of the oldest structures in southwestern China.

Leaning Tower of Pisa

Location: Pisa, Italy
Years built: 1173-1399 CE
The Leaning Tower of Pisa is a bell tower, a type of tower built to hold a bell. It belongs to the Pisa Cathedral, a Catholic church. The tower has eight stories. There are almost 300 steps inside to access the top story, where seven bells are located. The Leaning Tower of Pisa is famous for its tilt, which was an accident. The ground underneath it was made up of sand and clay. It was so soft that the tower's foundations were not stable. The tower started to lean while it was still being constructed. It leaned more and more as it got taller, and it kept leaning after it was completed. Many architects and engineers tried to stop the tilt. As of 2008, the Leaning Tower of Pisa is stable.

Minaret of Jam

Location: Shahrak District, Afghanistan
Years built: approximately 1190 CE

A minaret is a narrow tower usually located near a mosque. The Minaret of Jam is 213 feet (65 meters) tall. It has turquoise inscriptions on it with text from the Quran. The ruins near the Minaret of Jam suggest that it might have been part of the lost city of Turquoise Mountain. A lost city is a city from the past that has been uninhabited for so long that people forgot where it was located. Turquoise Mountain is believed to be one of the greatest cities of its time and tolerant of different religions.

Interior of Minaret Jam

DO YOU KNOW ABOUT...

How Big is the Tower's Tilt?

Over the years, the Leaning Tower of Pisa's tilt has been reduced from 5.5 degrees to 4 degrees. The high side of the tower is 186 feet (56.7 meters) tall and the low side is 183 feet (55.9 meters) tall. The top of the tower is almost 13 feet (4 meters) away from where its position would be if it were straight.

Leaning Tower of Pisa

Eiffel Tower

Location: Paris, France
Years built: 1887-1889 CE

The Eiffel Tower was built for the World's Fair in 1889, an event where different countries display things like technology, art, and cultural objects. The Eiffel Tower is 1,063 feet (324 meters) tall. It was built from thousands of pieces of iron in a lattice design. Until 1930, it was the tallest structure in the world. The Eiffel Tower has three levels. The lower two levels have restaurants, and the top level is an observation deck. About seven million people visit the Eiffel Tower every year. The Eiffel Tower lights up at night. It is used for transmitting radio and television signals.

Skyscrapers

A skyscraper is a very tall building that usually has more than forty floors and is at least 500 feet (152.4 meters) tall. Skyscrapers taller than 984 feet (300 meters) are called supertall skyscrapers.

Carlton Centre

Location: Johannesburg, South Africa
Years built: 1967-1973 CE
The Carlton Centre is currently the second tallest building in Africa. When it was first built, it was the tallest building in the southern hemisphere. It is 732 feet (223 meters) tall and has fifty floors. It is made of light brown concrete. Inside, the Carlton Centre has offices and a shopping center. On the top floor, there is an observation deck for viewing the city. Sometimes this floor is called the "top of Africa."

Empire State Building

Location: New York, United States
Years built: 1930-1931 CE
The Empire State Building is 1,454 feet (443.2 meters) tall and has 102 stories. It was constructed in just eleven months! It was the tallest building in the world when it was built. Today it is the 28th-tallest building. It holds offices for about 1,000 businesses. The 86th and 102nd floors have observation decks. The Empire State Building is an art deco building. Art deco is a style popular in the 1920s and 1930s that involves geometric patterns, modern materials, and metallic colors.

Entrance Hall

Taipei 101

Location: Taipei, Taiwan
Years built: 1999-2004 CE
Taipei 101 is 1,667 feet (508 meters) tall and has 101 stories. It is one of the fifteen tallest buildings in the world. It was designed to look like a bamboo stalk. It is tiered, like a pagoda. Taipei 101 has very powerful elevators. They can travel from the fifth floor to the 89th floor in just forty seconds. The first five floors of the skyscraper are malls, and the 88th, 89th, and 91st floors have an observation deck. Taipei 101 lights up every New Year's Eve and puts on a fireworks show.

Q1

Location: Gold Coast, Australia
Years built: 2002-2005 CE

The Q1, or Queensland Number One, is the tallest building in Oceania. It is 1,058 feet (322.5 meters) tall and has seventy-eight stories. It is made mostly of concrete, steel, and glass. Q1 is a residential building, which means people live in it in apartments. There is an observation deck on the top two floors called SkyPoint. It is the only observation deck on the beach in all of Australia. You can reach SkyPoint in two ways: taking the high-speed elevator for forty-three seconds or climbing 1,331 steps.

DO YOU KNOW ABOUT...

Green Buildings

Taipei 101 is the tallest green building in the world. A green building is a building that uses resources efficiently and is environmentally friendly. To qualify, a building must meet requirements in not only its design and construction, but also throughout its use and when it is demolished.

Taipei 101

Gran Torre Santiago

Location: Santiago, Chile
Years built: 2006-2013 CE

The Gran Torre Santiago is the tallest building in South America. It is 984 feet (300 meters) tall and has sixty-four stories, not counting six underground basement floors. The shadow of the building is more than a mile (1.6 kilometers) long. The Gran Torre is mostly made of concrete, steel, and glass. There are more than twenty-four elevators in the building. The 61st and 62nd floors of the skyscraper are an observation deck called Sky Costanera.

Megatall Skyscrapers

A megatall skyscraper is a skyscraper that is more than 1,969 feet (600.2 meters) tall. There are currently only three megatall skyscrapers in the world, but there are more under construction. Currently, all of them are located in Asia.

Burj Khalifa

Location: Dubai, United Arab Emirates
Years built: 2004-2009 CE

The Burj Khalifa is the tallest building in the world. It is 2,716.5 feet (827 meters) tall and has more than 160 stories. It is so tall that more than forty tests were needed to make sure it would be sturdy in windy weather. The facade of the Burj Khalifa is made of aluminum and glass. The skyscraper was designed with setbacks. A setback is a place where the wall moves back, forming a step or ledge. The setbacks mean the building gets narrower as it gets taller. Inside, the Burj Khalifa contains a hotel, luxury apartments, offices, decks, and facilities for residents, like swimming pools and a library.

DO YOU KNOW ABOUT...

The Tallest Building of the Future

After 2020, the Burj Khalifa might lose its status as the tallest building in the world. A skyscraper called Jeddah Tower is being built in Saudi Arabia. It is planned to be 3,280 feet (999.7 meters) tall—that's 236 feet (72 meters) taller than the Burj Khalifa. Jeddah Tower is planned to have more than 200 stories and the highest observation deck in the world at more than 2,000 feet (610 meters).

Makkah Royal Clock Tower

Location: Mecca, Saudi Arabia
Years built: 2004-2011 CE

The Makkah Royal Clock Tower is the third-tallest building in the world. It is one of seven skyscraper hotels in the complex Abraj Al-Bait. The clock tower is 1,972 feet (601 meters) tall and has 120 stories. The other six towers have forty-two to forty-eight stories. The clock itself is more than five times larger than Big Ben's clock in Westminster Palace. Abraj Al-Bait is located right across the street from the Great Mosque of Mecca. People often stay in its hotels when making pilgrimages to the mosque.

Shanghai Tower

Location: Shanghai, China
Years built: 2008-2014 CE

The Shanghai Tower is the second-tallest building in the world. It is 2,073 feet (632 meters) tall and has 127 stories. The Shanghai Tower has a glass facade with two layers. In between the layers, there are atriums with gardens and restaurants. The result is like nine buildings stacked on top of each other, enclosed with glass. These nine zones cannot be seen from outside the building because of the outer layer of glass. The Shanghai Tower is an example of green architecture. It uses geothermal and wind energy and has indoor gardens to improve the quality of the air. Its twisted design reduced the amount of materials needed and the wind pressure on the building.

Glossary

Accessible – able to be used, especially by people with disabilities

Acoustics – qualities of a room that affect how well sound can be heard

Administrative – having to do with the management of something

Amphitheater – a round open building or arena for entertainment

Annex – a smaller building that is used as an extension of a larger building

Archaeology – the study of humans of the past using their artifacts and remains

Architecture – the practice of building a specific building style or a building project itself

Astronomer – a scientist who studies objects outside the earth's atmosphere like stars and planets

Atrium – an open or well–lit room in the center of a building

Balcony – a raised platform that projects out from the side of a wall

Cantilever – something that projects out and is supported at only one end

Client – someone who pays a person or company for a service

Collaboration – working together

Complex – a group of buildings that are related to each other

Composer – someone who writes music

Construction – the process of building something

Crypt – an underground chamber

Crystallize – to form crystals

Deity – a god

Demolish – to destroy an object

Denomination – a subgroup of a religion

Design – the process of planning or sketching the way something will look or work

Encase – to surround something with something else

Excavate – to uncover something by digging

Exhibit – something on display in an art gallery or museum

Facade – the front of a building

Fortify – to make stronger or safer

Gallery – a room or area with exhibits

Gladiator – a person who fights in public for other people's entertainment

Grove – a small group of trees

Handicraft – making things with one's hands

Helipad – a place where a helicopter lands and takes off

Inscription – an engraving or writing found on an object or building

Integrate – to unite two or more different things in one new thing

Landscape – an area of land; scenery

Lattice – a design involving strips of wood or metal that are crossed over each other

Lodging – a place to live or stay temporarily

Minaret – a tower of a mosque

Nave – the main part of a church

Oceania – the land in the central and southern Pacific Ocean

Pharaoh – a ruler of ancient Egypt

Pilgrimage – a journey to a holy place

Platform – a flat surface next to train tracks where people board a train

Plumbing – a system of moving water through a building

Portico – a row of columns with a roof at the entrance of a building

Proscenium – the wall and arch on a stage that separate the audience from the stage

Relief – a type of sculpture where the designs are raised from but still attached to the background

Remains – a dead body

Renaissance – a period of time in Europe from the 1300s to 1600s when art and science were popular; a style based on this time

Replica – an exact copy, typically on a smaller scale

Sediment – natural material deposited by wind or water

Translucent – clear enough to let light through but not enough to see through

Transparent – clear enough to see through

Ventilation – the movement of fresh air in a room or building

Index